WOMANS SHOES A MANS PERSPECTIVE

Gregory Cowper

AuthorHouse™
1663 Liberty Drive
Bloomington, IN 47403
www.authorhouse.com
Phone: 1-800-839-8640

First published by AuthorHouse 5/25/2010

ISBN: 978-1-4490-8495-0 (e)
ISBN: 978-1-4490-8493-6 (sc)

Library of Congress Control Number: 2010901953

Printed in the United States of America
Bloomington, Indiana

This book is printed on acid-free paper.

PREFACE

Woman's Shoes a Man's Perspective;" was a project I developed one weekend with my wife Teresa, while I was rummaging through the closets at the house and was stumbling on her shoes. I did a quick count and the number was about forty pairs.

The math just didn't add up as I know my baby has an affliction for shoes, and over the twenty or so years we have been together; there have been more than forty pairs passing through our hallowed closets.

I asked her, "Where are all the shoes? I know you have more." I am sure all us men get the same blank look and wry smile; as if through telepathy we are suppose to know where they all go.

I then said to her; "a man should write a lighthearted book about women's shoes, from a man's perspective."

A fun and humorous account of the psychology of women and shoes! A guide for the men in this world, who have experienced the foibles of their women, and their shoes! ' If only for the sake of naming all the shoes; because there is a whole sub-culture and dictionary of names for all the different shapes and styles of shoes.'

My wife and I sat down and prepared a questionnaire that we could circulate to women in her realm of social and business life. Business Women, mothers, and single girls, of all ages and cultures; and from different walks of life!

The idea being that the responses would give us a good guide for ascertaining the truth about their association with one of the hottest topics in a woman's life….her shoes.

If not for the contribution from all these women, this book would not have the bite and conviction from the woman's perspective. i.e. The truth about their association with shoes. I would like to thank all those women who participated in the project, and hope that you find a little humor in our finished product.

I would also like to thank my wife Teresa and my daughter Geraldine for giving me the inspiration to write the book. Watching them all these years and their association with shoes, gave me the idea for the book. They are both different personalities and have a totally different taste in adorning their feet.

I would also like to invite all women who have the opportunity to read this dissertation, to visit our website and continue this saga of the woman's shoe.

Through the website we hope you will complete the questionnaire and post it for others to read. We will have contests for the best stories about your shoes. We also have a daily live platform modeling of new shoes being released in the market. You will be able to view live models showing off the shoes, and I might add models of all shapes and sizes. Hence, no matter who you are; you will be able to see what the shoes look like on a woman like yourself before buying.

So please go to www.wsmpshoes.com and begin the saga.

INTRODUCTION

I begin this journey into the fascinating analysis of women's shoes, to determine what motivates a woman to have an inordinate number of shoes in her wardrobe. The average man consoles himself with maybe five pairs of shoes….he buys his shoes for functionality. Two dress shoes, maybe a pair of casual loafers, some boots to bring out the man in him, the house and yard strollers, and of the course the sports shoes.

A woman however, does not look at the shoe as an item of clothing, or as a functional means to cover her feet from the grime of the road. The shoe to her is an art form, a means to express herself, an extension of her emotional self. "The shoe is the next best thing to having an orgasm; and maybe not in some cases."

Like most men, I have always tried to ascertain why women have to have so many shoes. The shoes are so important that they dictate how many rooms in a house are needed. When looking at buying a new house, the woman always checks out the closet space. I've heard women say; "and that's plenty of space to keep my shoes." Have you seen yourself relegated to a tiny corner of the closet?" if you are lucky. Have you seen your meager assortment moved closer and closer to the front door? Can you even find them sometimes?

I decided that (we) men needed to present a lighthearted analysis of the woman's shoe, after years and years of watching the beautiful little beasties coming and going into my life. Finding boxes hidden under the beds, in closets and bundled up in plastic bags in the garage!

Wondering where all these new shoes go? Is there a shoe heaven; how come the house is not full of all these shoes. "Why I never see them leave the front door, when they have exhausted their little life-spans?"

I have watched my wife and daughters shoes come and go over the years, which prompted me to write this short dissertation on the " Man's perspective, " to woman's shoes.

Contents

THE QUESTIONNAIRE

To undertake my analysis, I decided that a questionnaire was needed so that I could ascertain the different motives of various women and their fascination with shoes. I solicited the help of my wife to circulate my questions among her peers and friends in her realm of business and social life.

In the next section of this book I have included the answers to this questionnaire from an assortment of the women who participated. I recommend all women to go to our website and fill in the questionnaire for some fun, and post it for all to view. Share with us your feelings about shoes and the experiences you have had.

We have also underlined each question here in the book, so you can jot down your notes and observations; as a record for you to compare with the other women. The questionnaire was as follows:-

1. How many pairs of shoes do you currently own?

_____

_____

2. How many pairs of shoes do you buy each year? Please give your best estimate.

_____

_____

3. How many times each month do you wear the same shoes?

_____

_____

4. What makes you decide that you need a new pair of shoes? Is it when you see them? Is it to make you feel better? Is it based on new styles or fashion? Please describe.

_____

_____

5. What type of shoes do you like? Clogs, mules, pumps, Flats, Wedges, Boots Etc. Please describe.

_____

_____

6. When do you decide that your old shoes no longer meet your needs? i.e. When they are totally worn out, or can they still be worn?

_____

_____

7. What do you do with your old shoes? Do you throw them out, do you donate them, do you store them in a trophy cabinet?

_____

_____

8. Do you share your shoe purchases with your spouse/significant other? Or do you hide them?

_____

_____

9.   Do you share your shoe purchases with your girlfriends?

_____

_____

10. Do you have sex when wearing your shoes?

_____

_____

11. How do you store your shoes? Are they on racks; in original boxes; or clear plastic bins?

_____

_____

12. How do you decide on which pair of shoes to wear with an outfit? Is it based on color, style and mood?

_____

_____

13. What is the most amount of money you have spent on a pair of shoes? What is the least amount of money you have spent?

_____

_____

14. Do you have shoes that you purchased and never worn? How long have you had them?

_____

_____

15. If you find a shoe that you like, do you buy it in multiple colors?

_____

_____

16. Have you ever bought shoes that were not your size, but you just had to have them; and you made them fit?

_____

_____

17. Do you buy shoes for comfort or style?

_____

_____

18. Do you accessorize your shoes? Do you buy handbags, jewelry etc to match?

_____

_____

19.   Have you bought a pair of shoes that does not match any of your outfits, but you " had to have them." As a result have you gone and bought clothes to match?

_____

_____

20. When you travel on business or vacation; what is the average number of shoes you take?

_____

_____

21. Please share a great shoe story that will forever be implanted in your mind. i.e. Do you remember the shoes you were wearing on your first kiss? When you were proposed to? Did you fight someone over a pair of shoes?

_____

_____

_____

_____

_____

_____

_____

THE ANSWERS!!!

Question 1.

How many pairs of shoes do you currently own?

Answers.
Question 1.

How many pairs of shoes do you currently own?

Answers.

1. 45 (That's not too bad, right? Luckily you asked me this after I did my spring cleaning…I tossed at least 8 pairs of shoes then….. some.

2. 2.45-50

3. 28

4. Twenty

5. 40

6. 53

7. At least 50, typically a 50/50 seasonal split..

8. I don't know. Fifty?

9. I own at least 75 pairs of shoes including boots and athletic shoes.

10. Honestly if I had to guess I would say easily over 200..

11. About 75..

12. At least 40

13. 25.

14. Approx 100.

15. 50.

16. 45-50.

17. 30.

18. 50.

19. 68.

20. Twenty..

21. 50-60..

22. I would guess I have somewhere between 50-60 pairs.

23. 5.

24. 100.

25. 40.

26. About 100 or so.

Question 2.

How many pairs of shoes do you buy each year? Please give best estimate.

Answers

1. 12?

2. 7-12

3. 7

4. Five

5. 6

6. 12

7. Weeee!!!!!, at least a pair a month.

8. Approximately 5 or 6

9. I buy at least one pair of shoes each month.

10. Are you kidding, you want me to actually put this in writing? 20,30 ? Does that sound right?

11. Probably around 12

12. 10

13. 8

14. Approx 7

15. 10

16. 12

17. 9

18. 10

19. Five

20. Usually 10 or so...however with the economy I have cut down a lot.

21. 4-5 pairs per year

22. 5

23. 10

24. 6

25. 10-12

Question 3

How many times each month do you wear the same shoes?

Answers

1. Practical shoes: During the school year, I have 2-3 pair of comfortable shoes that I wear every day to work. During the summer, I have 2-3 pair of flip flops that I wear about every day. Impractical Shoes: Might happen to wear the same shoes two or three times a month.

2. 3 in the fall/winter. Once or twice in the summer/spring.

3. At most probably 10

4. Three

5. 8

6. 10

7. Depends on how many times I wear said outfit generally purchased for matching shoes

8. During the cold months, maybe 8. During the warm months, far less

9. I wear the same shoes at least 8 times a month. This would be my athletic shoe that I "teach" group exercise in

10. Tennis shoes to the gym, daily. Does this count? The nice crap that you probably based your question on maybe 4 or 5

11. Every time I run or play soccer, I obviously wear the same shoes. To work, I probably wear the same shoes about 12 times a month (black pumps). When I go out at night I mix it up much more!!

12. Depending on the season. Sandals and open toe are only in warm weather and that can be several times a week. In cold weather, I wear boots or booties 3 to 4 times a week.

13. Many times

14. Approx 7

15. 5

16. 5

17. 8- for the more commonly worn pairs

18. 12-15

19. Three

20. 12-15

21. I have one pair in particular that I wear at least 3 times per week

22. 4

23. 20 plus

24. 8

25. Several pairs get several wearings

Question 4.

What makes you decide that you need a new pair of shoes? Is it when you see them? Is it to make you feel better? Is it based on new styles or fashion? Please describe.

Answers

1. First of all, why do you need a reason?! Yes to all of the questions above, and I guess...* buying new clothes- you need the perfect shoes for the perfect outfit, right? * End/ beginning of season sales. * Good deal-coupons, discounts, sales. * Definitely when I see them-I think a lot of shoe shopping is done when there is no real need for a specific pair of shoes. I'm sometimes just looking for new shoes. * Special event (wedding, party, nice dinner, date, vacation or trip somewhere. Taking the dog for a walk. You know any good excuse.

2. All of the above and more! Shoe shopping is the best retail therapy because regardless of your body shape and size you can ALWAYS find a perfect pair of shoes!

3. Usually when I see them, but sometimes based on new styles.

4. New style-new season.

5. Unless I need something specific, I buy a pair of shoes when I see them and like them.

6. Just as I see them.

7. This question was obviously written by a man, to understand what makes you buy anything is to understand the concept of shopping in general. Men generally think they need a new pair of shoes because the black, brown or athletic shoe they own is falling apart. They go, generally begrudgingly, to the store, focused on the one thing they are looking for, find it, buy it (don't even always try it on!) and are out the door. The entire process taking no more than 20 minutes tops (and that's if there is a line at the register.) Women don't always even know if they need shoes they may be shopping for a comforter.... Which is next to the casual wear department... where there is a sale going on. While we didn't know we needed a new outfit, the opportunity to SPAVE (spending $50 and coming away with $150 of happy) was overwhelming. Now having this new outfit, or possibly multiple outfits, doesn't always mean you have the correct shoes (or purse for that matter) therefore, now you need to go shoe shopping. However, that's not really that simple either because once you get into the shoe store, there could be additional SPAVING opportunities. This could, does and has become a viscous circle.

8. When I see a pair I like.

9. All of the above are reasons or excuses for buying shoes.

10. All of the above.

11. Sometimes when I see them, sometimes there is a shoe that is trendy that I just really like; it is rare that I actually need

them! I don't really buy shoes to make me feel better, but it always does!

12. Most of the time , I'm looking for something specific- spring sandals, boots etc. Other times you just see a pair of shoes you must have because they are pretty sexy. New shoes always make me feel better.

13. You need to buy new shoes each season and then sometimes mid-season when you see others you have to have.

14. Usually when I see something cute and potentially comfortable.

15. When I see them.

16. When I see a pair I like and they have them to fit my size 11 foot…I purchase them.

17. If they look fashionable, unique, or would be good for work I have to snatch them up. If it meets my picky criteria (height, heel type, comfort, stability, style, fit. price) then I can't miss out on the opportunity.

18. Sometimes it is the need for a particular color or style to go w/ certain outfits-it gets put on the shopping list. But most of the time, it is seeing a pair and then creating the " need " for them.

19. New style new season.

20. I really don't need them I just see them and like the style and fit.

21. When I see them; when I see similar pairs on other women and I like them; when the fashion changes.

22. When they are on sale.

23. Usually for an event is when I buy new shoes.

24. Unless I need something specific, I buy a pair of shoes when I see them and like them.

25. Yes, if I like them or the style (and have the money especially if they are not full price.)

Question 5.

What type of shoes do you like? Clogs, mules, pumps, flats, wedges, boots etc. Please describe.

Answers

1. Flats for school. Heels or wedges for pretty much everything else

2. Definitely a boot fan here!

3. I am partial to mules, occasionally pumps (out of business necessity), rarely flats, and boots only seasonally

4. Slip on

5. I like all of the above

1. Wedges

2. All of the above, including but not limited to sandals of all types, flip flops (both casual and dress FF's), stilettos (ah those WERE the days), athletic shoes (I would say sneakers or tennis shoes but then you would know my roots), shoes with toe cleavage (low throats), and don't even get me started on the varying types of heels that are considered in the overall selection

3. Strappy sandals and sling back pumps

4. All of above! The question is what type of shoes do you dislike and the answer is "none"

5. Pumps-pointy toes, patent leather, high heels because they are sexy!!!! AND strappy high heeled sandals-all colors

6. Pumps, wedges, boots, flats, strappy sandals

7. I love high heel boots and booties in winter. I love high heel sandals and mules. I'm a child of the 70's and flat shoes are

just ugly and should be worn when grocery shopping or an outside casual event when you're walking in grass

8. Wedges- with fat heel and nice in-step and boots

9. I'm more of a comfy trendy flats person but do love my heels for the late date nights

10. Flats

11. Flats, pumps, heels, sneakers, boots, flip flops, sandals... anything except those ugly clogs. Do not own clogs

12. Love wedges!

13. At only 5'2" I am a pump girl. I love boots too but they must have a heel on them. Even my flip flops are stacked

14. Slip on

15. I love clogs (Dansko's especially), Uggs, rainbow sandals for the summer, and an assortment of flats

16. Sling back pumps are my favorite

17. I love pumps, but I own 25 pair of flip flops...in all colors and design

18. Flats, wedges, boots, sandals, rainbows, dansko's

19. I like all of the above

20. Pumps and flats mostly but my rainbows are "queen" here at the beach in the summer. I also like designer flip flops in many colors

Question 6.

When do you decide your old shoes no longer meet your needs? I.e. When they are totally worn out, or can they still be worn?

Answer

1. If I haven't worn them in over 2 years or they are totally worn out

2. Totally worn out (and even then I keep them for at least a year or two after that- they become your friends

3. Totally worn out

4. Sole falling off

5. I get rid of some of my common shoes when they are worn out. Others I get rid of due to the style

6. They can still be worn, but do not look smart enough for me

7. I've had very few shoes actually wear out, that's a man thing. Again, because instead of 3 pairs of shoes you wear every day of your life, we have options therefore decreasing the possibility of wearing them out

8. When I find a pair I like better in the same color

9. I donate my shoes to charity because they are in good shape when I get done with them

10. Both

11. Totally worn out or out of style

12. Either they wear out or I just don't like them anymore

13. When I get sick of them, feel they are out of style, or not comfortable

14. I get rid of shoes that have given me blisters in the past or if I know I won't wear it in the next year

15. Donate them

16. When the heels are worn down to nails, when the soles are coming off. I get my money's worth out of a pair of shoes

17. Take them to the consignment shop or donate them

18. If I didn't wear the shoes the entire season prior then it is deemed "give-away." For my favorite shoes, I go the extra step and take them to the shoe doctor to be repaired when they get a bit worn. Once repairs are no longer helpful I say goodbye

19. Donate them if still in decent shape, if not throw them away

20. They can still be worn (sometimes practically brand new) I just get tired of looking at them and want new ones-that's pitifull!!!!

21. When they are totally worn out; when they no longer are fashionable; when I change my mind for whatever reason

22. They get rotated to the back and sit there until they come back in style

23. When even the shoe repair guy shakes his head

24. I get rid of some of my common shoes when they are worn out. Others I get rid of due to style

25. Some are worn out, others have lost their fashion savvy or I no longer have an outfit to match cuz I gained too much weight or the outfit is ruined etc, I cannot find anything to match them anymore or just need to weed some out to make room for more

Question 7.

What do you do with your old shoes? Do you throw them out, do you donate them, do you store them in a trophy cabinet?

Answers

1. I throw out the well worn shoes and donate the gently worn shoes. I have hung on to a few pairs of shoes that I know I will never wear again, but just can't seem to part with them

2. Most I throw out. However, I did keep a pair of shoes in a box at the top of my closet for close to ten years as I could not bring myself to get rid of them!

3. Sometimes donate them, but they are usually too worn out

4. Donate them if still in decent shape, if not, throw them away

5. If the shoe is badly worn I trash it. If not too badly worn I donate it. I don't have any trophy shoes however my 22 yr old daughter has two pairs that she actually has on a shelf in her bedroom. The shoes are so great it looks good in her single bedroom. Everyone that visits her place makes a remark about that idea

6. Donate them

7. Mostly I either give them away or donate them to charitable foundation. I must admit, there are a few that are trophy case worthy but that's because of the memory associated with said shoe

8. After maybe 3 or 4 years, I donate them if they're not too worn

9. I donate my shoes to charity because they are in good shape when I get done with them

10. Donate them to a woman's shelter

11. Donate them to Goodwill

12. Some that are past the point of repair I toss. All others I give to charity

13. I have some old shoes in my closet that I never wear but can't seem to let go…the one's I am sick of…they get thrown out

14. I give them to the cleaning lady because either she can use them or knows someone that can use them

15. Donate them

16. I throw them away..it hurts..but I do throw away shoes about once a year

17. Take them to the consignment shop or donate them

18. I donate all my old shoes!

19. Donate them if still in decent shape, if not, throw them away

20. Donate them or sell them at yard sale

21. I typically donate them to a place like salvation army

22. Thrift shop donation

23. I donate them. I can't afford the expensive ones yet (aka jimmy Choo) but when I do, they will probably go to a special place in my home

24. Donate them to charity

25. Either throw them out or donate them

Question 8

Do you share your shoe purchases with your spouse/significant other? Or do you hide them?

Answers

1. I always share, but I think he couldn't care less

2. I don't just share-I model every pair!!!

3. Usually hide them, but he ALWAYS notices when I have something new

4. Yes

5. For the most part I don't share my purchases with my husband. Not that I hide them because often the box in a bag is in the open for him to see if he wanted. After living with me and 3 daughters, he just goes with the flow. Shoes, clothes etc

6. Show

7. Depends if he's home when I arrive with my purchases. Generally IF they are commented on as "are those new" I've already worn them at least once, hence no they are not

8. When I was married, I usually hid them

9. My boyfriend doesn't get the pleasure I get from buying new shoes. Therefore, I keep it to myself.

10. Are you kidding? I hide them. Unfortunately I was at the shoe store one day with my husband (I know bad mistake) and there was a lady checking out in front of us that was buying 5-6 pairs of shoes and telling the clerk NOT to put the boxes in the bag, just the shoes. That way she could just throw them in the back of her car and take in a pair daily without her husband noticing. Moral of the story: Do NOT take your husband into a shoe store!!

11. n/a

12. When I was married I always shared my purchases and told him what a good buy they were because they were on sale. A great trick I learned from my mother.

13. I share! I spent $120 on three pairs this week (bargain!) and brought them home and showed them off and had to tell why I had to buy them

14. He basically finds out when I put them on and he notices something different, then I tell him that I bought it ages ago! Haha

15. I am single

16. Don't have a significant other!!! Can buy all the shoes I want, when I want and spend what I want. No need to hide!!!!

17. I will definitely show off my new shoes. I have not hid my purchases with the exception of maybe once or twice

18. I share my joy with others-including my spouse

19. Yes

20. Ok, you aren't quoting anyone are you? Sometimes I share and sometimes I don't…just all depends on his mood

21. Generally share them with my spouse

22. Are you kidding? Some are still in the trunk of the car!

23. Depends on how many pairs I bring home on that day. There is a line where he might start asking questions

24. Most of the time share but he just rolled his eyes

25. Sometimes…I try to come home when football is on.

Question 9.

Do you share your shoe purchases with your girlfriends?

Answer

1. Absolutely!

2. Absolutely-even my doctor-we swap stories?

3. Yes, especially if I got a great deal

4. Only if I get a good deal

5. Sometimes, usually when I'm wearing them and they ask about them

6. Yes

7. As in do I share a great sale story, always, it's the code of the west

8. Mostly with my sister

9. If I get a terrific deal, then of course I share this with my sisters/girlfriends!

10. No

11. Sometimes, but often times you don't want them to have the same ones so you don't want to tell them all bout them

12. Of course

13. Not really…only if they notice and say "cute shoes."

14. I love to brag if I found a great deal especially! But if I over paid for them, I lie about what I paid

15. Yes

16. We all compare shoes

17. No

18. Of course, especially when you find a shoe for a fabulous price?

19. Only if I get a good deal

20. No, not really unless they notice

21. Sometimes

22. Only when I model them at the next get together

23. Not usually unless they are witness's to the purchase

24. Of course!

25. Occasionally

Question 10.

Do you have sex when wearing your shoes?

Answers

1. I think every girl has a pair or two of TMDFMQ shoes. These shoes might tend to stay on

2. No

3. No, always been afraid I would impale him with my heel

4. No

5. No

6. No

7. Have you heard of CFMP's

8. No

9. No

10. No

11. n/a

12. Of course

13. I have

14. My husband wishes…. ha!

15. No

16. Nope

17. No

18. If the opportunity arises….

19. No

20. No..

21. Huh? No

22. What?! Ruin my new shoes in the hot tub?

23. Tried once but injured my husband

24. No

25. Have thought about it?

Question 11.

How do you store your shoes? Are they on racks; in original boxes; or clear plastic bins?

Answer

1. Racks, original boxes

2. Boots are in original boxes until my husband builds the organizer I designed specifically for them. Sneakers are in a pile at the bottom of the closet. The rest are in numerous canvas shoe organizers (15 pair per organizer) canvas and wood with a handmade cloth "door" to prevent dust

3. On shelves in my closet or laundry room

4. Throw them in my shoe closet

5. All of the above, casual flip flop/tennis in shoe cubbies. Others in original boxes and some in clear plastic. I switch

6. On open racks so I can see them easily

7. All of the above, generally off season are in a separate room while current are close at hand

8. Some are in original boxes, some are in clear plastic bins

9. All of my closets are retrofitted to meet my needs. Therefore, my shoes are on shelves within my closet

10. In season are on racks. Out of season and formal shoes are in original boxes

11. Original boxes

12. No racks, bins or boxes. Lined up side by side in the closet

13. They are in laundry baskets in floor of closet…I have tried the original boxes thing, does not work for me

14. All on racks so I can see them better

15. Racks

16. Racks

17. They are mostly on wall racks and in a bin (for out of season shoes)

18. My in-season shoes are on shelves in my closet for easy view. My out of season shoes are stored in clear plastic boxes

19. Throw them in the closet, laundry room etc

20. In the original boxes or on racks

21. On racks; some in original boxes with digital photos taped to the end; clear plastic bins?

22. Racks

23. Nice shoes I store in individual shoe boxes, tennis shoes, dansko's etc go on racks

24. Racks-can fit more in small spaces

25. Racks, cubbies and clear bins…during the week tossed under the dresser..

Question 12.

How do you decide on which pair of shoes to wear with an outfit? Is it based on color, style or mood?

Answer

1. All of the above. That's why we girls have to get the opinion of others on our shoe choices

2. Mood then color

3. Color first, then style

4. Color and season

5. Color and style dictates which shoes I wear

6. All three

7. All of the above….

8. All three (color, style and mood).

9. All of the above apply

10. All of the above

11. Color and mood mostly

12. All of the above

13. All three...try them on with outfit and look in full length mirror

14. Everything has to be the right color for the outfit, and if I'm in the mood for comfy or trendy...

15. Mood

16. All of the above

17. In this order: color, occasion, mood

18. Color and style-mood takes a backseat to looking good!

19. Color and season

20. All 3

21. Color and style mostly. Mood can enter into it....

22. All of the above, its amazing the complexity of choosing which ones to wear..

23. Color and style

24. Some there is only one pair, others depend on where I am wearing that particular outfit that day

25. Mostly color, then mood.

Question 13.

What is the most amount of money you have spent on a pair of shoes? What is the least amount of money you have spent?

Answer.

1. $120 $5

2. The least amount-$3 for a wonderful pair of clogs I still wear. Most expensive $200 (that was before the wedding!!!)

3. Least amount id probably $15, most is $80

4. $100

5. Dress shoe-$225 Casual flip flop $15

6. $55 pound $1 pound

7. $200

8. The most I have spent on shoes is probably $150. The least I have spent is probably $20

9. $170

10. Most $500 (and they were on sale in London at Harvey Nichols 50% off!!!!) Least $5 on flip flops (do they count as shoes?)

11. Most $350-Black boots. Least-probably about $10

12. $129 is the most. $5 is the least

13. $55 $7

14. Least amount $10 and the most $400...jimmy Choos and Gucci's are irreplaceable.

15. $125 most. $15 least

16. $75 most. $5 least

17. $200 was the most. Least was 1 cent with a gift certificate

18. I'm a bargain shopper so the most I have paid for a pair of shoes was $90

19. $100

20. $150 & $20

21. The most I have spent was probably about $100; the least was about $10

22. $198......................$2.25

23. $5 dollars is the least. $ 220 is the most expensive

24. $160 that was rare. Usually it is under $40-$50, Rubber flip flops, $1

25. $160 most......$3 least

Question 14.

Do you have shoes that you have purchased and never worn? How long have you had them?

Answers

1. I've bought one pair of shoes that I absolutely loved, but never wore them out. I just didn't want to ruin them. I took them out every now and then and tried them on. I wore them at home sometimes when my boyfriend would make a nice candlelit dinner. I left them out one night and my dog chewed them to pieces. She must have known how much I loved them....

2. NO-sacrilege!

3. I have one particular pair of tennis shoes I think I wore one time, running the Peachtree

4. No

5. I bought a pair of brown boots in early Nov. They are still in the box so now I have to wait until next year

6. Yes, 2 years (but; they are ones that look like dressing up shoes, I had as a child; so I have them for a fancy dress opportunity!)

7. Nope

8. Sure. I've had them a few years

9. Lot's

10. Yes. And I have no idea!!!! Sometimes these are the ones I give away

11. Unfortunately, yes. I counted 5 pairs! That's bad. I have had one pair for about 3 ½ years, but one of them was only for a month and a half

12. No

13. Yes-shiny red shoes…one year

14. Yes, one pair I bought on biz trip last year

15. Yes- 2 years

16. es…had them 2 months. They are some strappy sandal/heels for summer…got a great buy…had to have them. Will wait for warm weather to wear them

17. Yes, usually 1 out of 10 shoes I buy is a bad purchase and I will wear them either once, twice or never

18. Some do not get worn much but they have all been worn at least once

19. No

20. No, I have worn all my shoes. I may not have worn them but once but I have worn them

21. No. I've worn some of them at least once

22. Yes, at least 8 years

23. No

24. No, but some I have only worn once

25. 5 years on one, 3 years for the other…

Question 15.

If you find a shoe that you like, do you buy it in multiple colors?

Answers

1. Absolutely!
2. Nah-that would be boring!
3. Only if I really like it and it's practical/comfortable
4. Yes
5. No
6. No
7. Always
8. I've known to do that
9. Yes, of course
10. Sometimes
11. Yes, sometimes. I have even bought two pair of the same shoe
12. Yes
13. Only sometimes
14. No, I usually force myself to decide on one and go with it
15. Sometimes
16. No
17. Yes, but seldom that has happened. If so, to have a pair in both black and brown
18. No, that is no fun! Got to mix up the styles
19. Yes
20. HAHA…yes

21. Yes

22. Only once, then they became very boring

23. Never

24. Sometimes

25. Nope…boring

Question 16.

Have you ever bought shoes that were not your size, but you just had to have them; and you made them fit?

Answers

1. Yes! They were too big, so I stuffed tissue in the toes. I also bought a pair of thong sandals with wedge heel that were too small, so I wore longer pants so people couldn't see my heel protruding from the back

2. Absolutely! My size range is 7.5 to 12…isn't everybody's? LOL

3. No, comfort and walkability is too big of an issue for me

4. Yes-but they hurt so bad that I ended up giving them away

5. No, I always buy my size. When you see someone in a shoe that doesn't fit you can tell right away

6. No

7. Of course, these shoes are known as sitting shoes

8. I did that when I was much younger

9. I have but have learned that it wasn't worth it

10. Hell no!!

11. Yes

12. No

13. No

14. Yup..!!! I allow myself to go up a size, and just use shoe padding. But never go a size smaller...OUCH

15. No

16. No

17. Yes, if it is half a size up or down

18. Yes. And my man the SHOE Doctor can stretch shoes and boots that are too small

19. Yes, but they hurt

20. Yes...BIG MISTAKE!!

21. No

22. Yes, Bunions, Bunions, Bunions!!!

23. Yes and my feet punished me for days

24. Yes, and I am usually sorry cuz it never really works out, even with shoe stretchers

25. Yes, and I can't walk for a week

Question 17,

Do you buy shoes for comfort or style?

Answers,

1. Style mostly, but I have to have comfortable shoes for work

2. Both, but mostly style

3. First for style, the comfort but comfort is a must

4. Style

5. Probably style first then comfort

6. Comfort, then style

7. Both

8. Both

9. All of the above

10. Both

11. 85%-style, 15%-comfort

12. Style

13. Both-that is why it is hard to find ones I like…when I do… HAVE to buy!

14. Both ideally

15. Comfort

16. The older I get…more for comfort. In my younger days… for style!!!

17. Yes, most all my shoes meet either of the criteria

18. Style! Comfort takes back seat w/mood

19. Style

20. I used to buy for style, now comfort

21. Style primarily, but comfort does enter in to it

22. Style

23. Style first and comfort a far second. Work shoes have a 50/50 relationship because I'm in sales and need to walk a lot

24. Both, it depends on the need

25. Comfort…mostly

Question 18.

Do you accessorize your shoes? Do you buy handbags, jewelry etc to match?

Answers.

1. No

2. Yuppers

3. Rarely

4. No

5. I don't match jewelry but often I do like my shoes and bag to match

6. No

7. Again, another man question, but of course, my addiction to shoes almost, but not quite, supercedes my addiction to handbags. Jewelry is an entirely separate questionnaire

8. Occasionally. I will usually buy a handbag to match dress shoes or special occasion shoes

9. Sometimes yes, but not always

10. Of course, doesn't everybody

11. Heck yeah!!!

12. Yes

13. Not really

14. Yes

15. No

16. Sometimes

17. That I don't do

18. I do have handbags and jewelry to match most of my shoes but I do not typically buy handbags just because they match my shoes. handbags have a life of their own

19. No

20. Sometimes…depends on if I bought the shoes for a special occasion or not

21. No

22. I have antique clips to use on them

23. No, I hate "matchy, matchy." It's not in style

24. Occasionally

25. Sometimes...if I see a good handbag

Question 19.

Have you bought a pair of shoes that does not match any of your outfits, but you "had to have them." As a result have you gone and bought clothes to match?"

Answers

1. Yes, to both

2. Isn't that accessorizing? LOL Absolutely

3. Yes, bought one pair of platinum metallic gray heels this winter and now I own three different shades of grey pants

4. Yes

5. I have definitely bought shoes with nothing to go with it. I had to search for the right outfit to go with the shoe instead of the other way around

6. No

7. Please refer to answer 4. " Now having this new outfit, or possibly multiple outfits, doesn't always mean you have the correct shoes (or purse for that matter) therefore, now you need to go shoe shopping.

8. Occasionally. I will usually buy a handbag to match dress shoes or special occasion shoes

9. This has happened to me in more than one occasion

10. Yes!!!!

11. Who hasn't!!!!

12. To match dress shoes or special occasion shoes

13. This has happened to me in more than one occasion

14. Yes!!!!

15. Who hasn't!!!!

16. Yes

17. Yes!!

18. Yes!!

19. No

20. Jeans go with anything!!!!

21. Yes, sometimes. When I buy a pair of shoes that has a unique color combination I will be on the lookout for matching outfits

22. Of course! Sometimes shoes make the outfit

23. Yes

24. Oh yes…

25. Yes… all the time

Question 20.

When you travel on business or vacation; what is the average number of shoes you take?

Answers.

1. Probably 2 pair for each day on average

2. Average 3 day trip-5 pair of shoes. Week-long trip-minimum of 8 pair

3. 3 pair

4. Two

5. Business 3-4. Vacation-5 or 6 pairs

6. 6 pairs

7. This completely depends on the length of the stay in question. Minimally 4, maximum, if driving, well there is no maximum, if flying maybe 6

8. It depends on what outfits I take. I take at least 4 pairs of shoes

9. When traveling by air, I limit the number of shoes to one casual, one athletic, and one dress. When traveling by car, I have no limit. Therefore, depending on how many days I will be gone, I could have a pair for each day

10. Business 5-10 depending on the length of the trip...then if I don't have enough time I go and buy more... Vacation is another story, I am getting ready for a cruise to Bermuda for 5 days and will probably take 20-25 pairs...sandals, evening, day, exercise, spa shoes, walking...you can NEVER have to many shoes

11. Business 3-4; vacation-depends on how long I am gone, but easily 6 or 7 for a long weekend

12. 4 pairs

13. 4 or 5

14. 5 pairs

15. 5

16. 4

17. Not too many, maybe 2 or 3 pairs. I try to do solely carry on as much as possible and it limits me greatly. I have started leaving backup pairs at regular vacation spots

18. I do well w/business trips-limiting my packed shoe count to 3. Vacations on the other hand....the limit depends on how

much room my husband will give me in his suitcase for some of my shoes

19. Two

20. 5-7

21. 2 pairs-on average

22. 5

23. Vacation anywhere up to 15 plus, business trips 5 or less. Just depending on the length of the trip

24. 5-6

25. It depends, by car, sea air or rail….there are options

QUESTION 21…PLEASE SHARE A GREAT SHOE STORY THAT WILL FOREVER BE IMPRINTED IN YOUR MIND.

I posed this question to all the ladies who participated in the questionnaire, as I wanted to see what great experiences, or foibles have affected women with shoes.

I felt this deserved its own chapter heading, as there were some great stories to tell!!!

ANSWERS

1. The first shoe story that comes to mind isn't about my own shoes but about some students at my school. Shoes are definitely more important to girls rather than guys... The fourth and fifth graders were announcing the winners of Field day over the intercom. The kids were heard cheering throughout the school for their teams. At the end of the long day, the teachers were exhausted and ready for dismissal to begin. One last announcement was delivered by our principal reporting that a fourth grade child was missing a pink sneaker. There must have been a mix up at the inflatable obstacle course where the kids had to take off their shoes. the

students were asked to check their shoes and classrooms for the missing shoe and report to the office if they had found it. Ten minutes later, still no pink shoe had been found. The principal made another announcement-almost laughing that a black shoe had been found, but we were still missing the pink shoe. She asked the teachers to check each child's feet for the missing shoe. Dismissal was being put on hold until the shoe was found. Finally, a teacher found a third grade boy wearing one pink shoe and one black shoe. Mystery solved! This just proves that shoes are more important to girls than boys.

2. When I was 19 I had just started having to pay for my own shoe habit and I had just purchased a pair of white leather knee length 2 inch heel boots. They were the absolute "bomb" and I shoveled out over $100 for these bad boys. I was wearing them for the 2nd maybe third time since purchase when I was in a pretty severe car accident. Luckily I was conscious when the paramedics got me out of the car and started assessing my condition as they were preparing to cut these boots off of me. I went ballistic! I threatened to sue the pants of the fire department, the hospital, the city, anyone and everyone if even one scratch was found on my boots. There I was with a broken leg, dislocated hip, a shattered shoulder and a concussion with who knows what else wrong; pulling these boots off myself so that they were not cut. Needless to say, my injuries all healed, and I proudly wore the boots on many more occasions!!!

3. No Comment

4. I did actually buy a pair of shoes that were blue/green spring shoes and they matched an outfit perfect but the size was ½ size smaller than I normally wear but I HAD to have them. I soaked a pair of cotton socks in rubbing alcohol (per a suggestion from friend), put them on my feet and then put the shoes on and walked around in the shoes for a while to "stretch" them out. Didn't work. Gave the shoes away and then since I could not find a pair of shoes that I liked in my size to match the outfit that I had bought, I gave the outfit away too.

5. My favorite story was when I was pretty young. Six grade to be exact. My mom being very traditional wanted me to wear dressy socks (no lacey ruffles but just as bad) with a dress shoe that I had beg to buy. I left the house in the socks, walking to school I took the socks off and hid them under a shrub. During school it snowed. That afternoon I had to retrieve the frozen socks, put them on and go home. My mom saw the wet socks in the laundry and asked about them. I had to tell her I stepped in a puddle. As you can see, my shoe adventures started at a very young age.

6. I remember wearing a pair of 6" high thigh length boots to work in the 70's and catching the heel on the curb at London Bridge Station, to end up sprawled in front of a row of London taxis!

7. My first kiss, likely a pair of sneakers, when I was proposed to, slippers, no fights. What is the best shoe story is that I, and my sister, both come by our addictions (shoes, clothes and handbags) honestly. Our father ran one of the largest shoe chains in the country. We had shoes in every color. My sister would wear the same shoes but one in each color to match an outfit. The insteps of our shoes said " made expressly for Karla." I have a job that occasionally requires that I tour manufacturing plants that require steel toe shoes; mine were made for me and are black suede w/hot pink piping. Generally plant managers will actually step on my toes because they don't believe they are actually steel toe shoes. You have to be careful because you can find yourself judging people by the shoes they wear (women I should say). A scuffed, dirty shoe???Never, a nail for a heel, dear god what were you thinking? Gum soles, hello, where's your walker? 6 inch stiletto on a 60 year old woman? C'mon mama, give it a rest, we can see your bunion's, on a 15 year old girl, where IS your MAMA? On a 20-30 year old girl, got a hot date. By the way, I have a guest bedroom and the décor theme.... shoes. My sister's guest room theme...flip flops. Best shoes ever....9 years old, paten leather black and red boots, white "go-go" boots, skimmers, tap shoes, back bow heels & HIGH heels of any kind!

8. I don't fight anyone over a pair of shoes. When I find a pair I like in my size and the store does not have many in my size, I will typically buy them to keep someone else from buying them before I make up my mind whether it's a good buy. I'm the same way about clothes.

9. The boots I had on for my first date with my "now" boyfriend made my "butt" look good. Therefore, I had to buy all colors. I still haven't worn the other "colors" and it has been five years. I teach group exercise in the mornings....6am in the morning. I used to have "every" color of typical business pumps all made by the same manufacturer. There were more than one occasion when I grabbed a navy and black in my gym bag and didn't realize until I was dressing at the gym. Sometimes I was able to go home and "fix" my mistake, and other times I was forced to wear my mistake! How many have had that happen to you?

10. See 8. Are you kidding? I hide them. Unfortunately I was at the shoe store one day with my husband (I know bad mistake) and there was a lady checking out in front of us that was buying 5-6 pairs of shoes and telling the clerk NOT to put the boxes in the bags, just the shoes. That way she could just throw them in the back of her car and take in a pair daily without her husband noticing. Moral of the story: DO NOT TAKE YOUR HUSBAND INTO A SHOE STORE!

11. I don't know if I really have any good shoe stories...sorry!

12. My aunt who was a school teacher always bought the most fabulously expensive, beautiful shoes and matching handbags. When I was a little girl she always let me wear them and play dress up. When I became a teenager, she would let me borrow shoes to go out on dates or out with my friends. She was definitely a shoe friend. She had Aigner shoes and matching bags, bandolino, Farragomo, Coach and many eelskin and Italian leather shoes from her travels to Europe and around the world. She knew how much I loved and appreciated her shoes and handbags so she left them to me in her will. I still cherish them.

13. Yellow keds when I was around eight years old..I loved those shoes and drew a picture of them when I was older...

14. No comment (check email not formatted)

15. I wore a flat shoe and a heel shoe to work which were also different colors. Did not realize until I went home.

16. No comment

17. The only time I was ever embarrassed about how many shoes I owned was when my father-in-law came to visit last year, saw my closet, and gasped in horror. He thought it was rather ridiculous. I didn't tell him I had more shoes stored away in a bin. In college I was in New York City with a very unique pair of mary jane style shoes and the owner of a famous clothing company saw me sitting outside a store and asked if he could photograph my shoes for inspiration for his next shoe collection. When the shoes were worn out I auctioned them on ebay and they sold for close to the full amount of money that the shoes originally cost.

18. My husband and I decided to take ballroom dancing lessons before our wedding. We wanted to learn a choreographed first dance to impress all our guests. I decided I needed a dance worthy shoe to wear with my gown. Of course due to my height it had to have a noteworthy heel, but this time comfort was also an important factor in finding the right pair. I found the perfect shoe in a color that matched my beautiful gown, a heel that was still danceable, and style that would keep my feet dancing comfortable for hours. I wore the wedding shoes during our lessons, and with every practice session in the studio, in the living room, and in the garage. The shoes would know the steps even if I forgot. The shoes were not with me when I said those memorable vows and kissed my groom for the first time, as we were married barefoot on the beach. But they were waiting anxiously for their appearance for our First Dance. The wedding shoes did not let me down! They glided , turned, and spinned effortlessly as we fancied our guests with an elegant Waltz that transitioned into a spicy tango! Two years later, the wedding shoes sit lovingly in a clear plastic shoe box at the top of my closet. On occasion I

catch a glimpse of them. They remind me of the many times my husband and I stepped on each other, laughed at each other, and enjoyed the quality time we spent with each other while learning a new skill. They recall the joy and fun we shared with the rest of our family and friends as we danced the night away after our ceremony. Last but not least, they inspire me to keep dancing with my husband until we are too old to enjoy it!

19. No comment

20. I used to love Birkenstocks because of the comfort issue and I probably had at the time about 4-5 pairs... My boss & friend (one in the same and will not mention anyone's name) talked about how ugly these shoes were that wearing the shoes gave me a complex so I donated all of the Birkenstocks I owned to Charity. I will never own another pair!!!

21. I wish I could help with this, but I honestly do not recall anything like this involving shoes.

22. Can't help you here, memories gone....

23. N/A

24. Finding a $200 pair of Ellen Tracy shoes (the only ones in the entire store and they were my size!!!) in the perfect odd (meaning hard to find) colors of sea green and turquoise that I needed to accompany my mother of the bride's dress (which I also got a steal-YES!) by a different designer to wear at one of my daughter's wedding and getting them for only $30!

25. My most memorable story was on a hot date in my twenties, rowing around on a pond with my boyfriend. We were starting to get hot and wild when one of my shoes fell off into the pond...now this was at night. You can imagine my dismay, and my poor boyfriend was cooled off very quickly; as he had the task of rowing furiously around the pond trying to find my shoe. Never did find the shoe... the moral of the story, "take your shoes off before getting in a boat, and lying on your back in the boat!!!!"

HOW MANY SHOES DOES SHE OWN?

The responses to my questionnaire were somewhat surprising, and gave me a good perspective on the personalities of women. What I did ascertain was that women on average buy at least twelve (12) pairs of shoes each year. That would be the consistent shopper who follows a strict routine. They methodically clean out their wardrobes and move out the old pairs with some routine.

The inconsistent shopper tends to buy in bunches, going out every quarter and stocking up with five to six pairs of shoes. They tend to gather up bunches of shoes which disappear into the back of the car.

Now if you analyze this purchasing routine and use the consistent shopper as an example, that would be one pair a month. When you apply some logical economics to the consistent shoe shopper, the numbers are quite staggering.

If you took the average life-expectancy, say 60 years and purchasing power of a woman; say 18 years. i.e. She starts buying her own shoes at age 18. You would average a total of 500 plus shoes in her lifetime.

Now to make it even more interesting, if you analyze the total contribution to the GDP of most countries by looking at income spent on woman's shoes over her lifetime (500 pairs), the number is staggering depending on the price of the shoe.

(1)At $40 per shoe, $20,160,

(2) at $60 per shoe $30,240,

(3) at $80 per shoe $40,320,

These are conservative prices for shoes, and I know that most women now are chuckling to themselves and saying where did this guy come from? To think I would buy a pair of shoes for $40, $50 even $80 bucks. Because we all know, or men should know that woman's shoes can go up to $1000 per pair.

Now from a man's perspective, if the woman in your life has expensive taste's and goes for the $200 dollar shoes, then you need to plan in your lifetime on budgeting approximately $100,000 for shoe purchases. All men need to study hard at college so you can look forward to spending all this money to keep your baby happy and contented.

I even look now at the cows, alligators etc and say to myself " You poor suckers."There is even a national restaurant chain that advertises eating more chicken. I would say in the ad, "wear-less-shoes?"

KNOWING YOUR SHOES

Most men need to appreciate the fairer sex, and to take a big step forward in understanding the many facets of the woman in your life. You need to also have a good appreciation of her shoes. Know her shoes, and you go a long way to knowing her.

Now this is a daunting undertaking; as there are so many different types of shoes. Men's shoes are basic…they are called shoes. We have dress shoes, sports shoes, boots and loafers. Women however, have created a whole new dictionary for their shoes. I have tried to present the various different variations of sometimes the same shoe. The many names, and the designs….have all been pictorially presented.

My wife has graciously modeled these shoes for all men to know; "what they are all called?" So next time when the wife, girlfriend, hooker or whatever in your life walks in the room…you can say, "that's a nice pair of………?"

FLIP FLOPS- STANDARD DESIGN

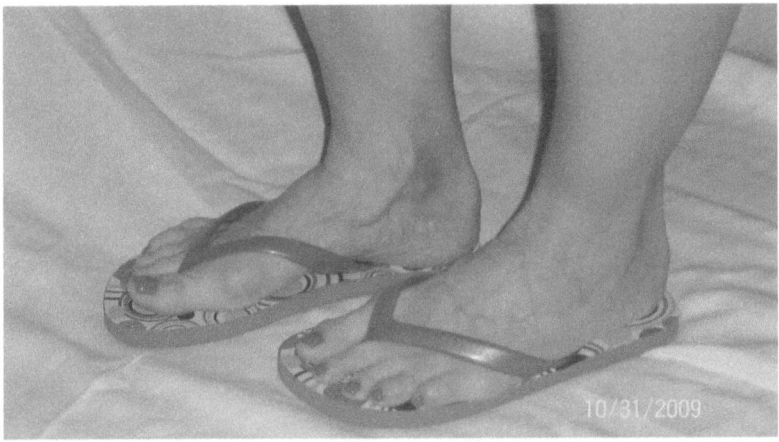

These are the traditional Flip Flop, designed for summer, the beach and loafing around the house..

FLIP FLOPS- FORM FITTED

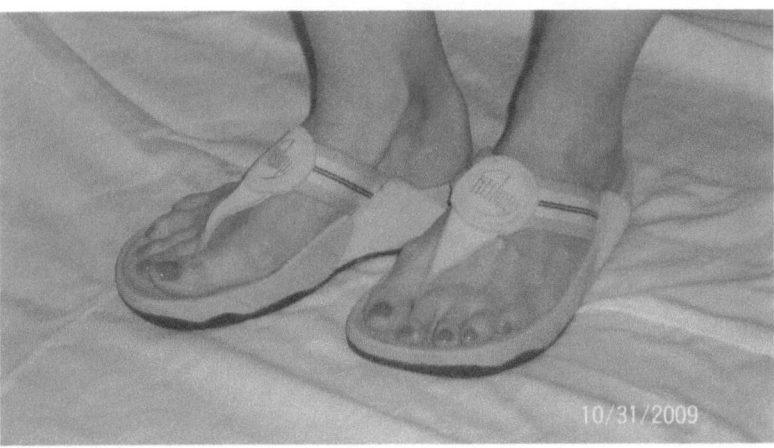

There are various designs of flip flops. These are the new design of comfort Flip Flops which have form fitted soles to give more stability and support. These new types of Flip Flops simulate walking in the sand and provide exercise of leg muscles.

WEDGE SANDALS

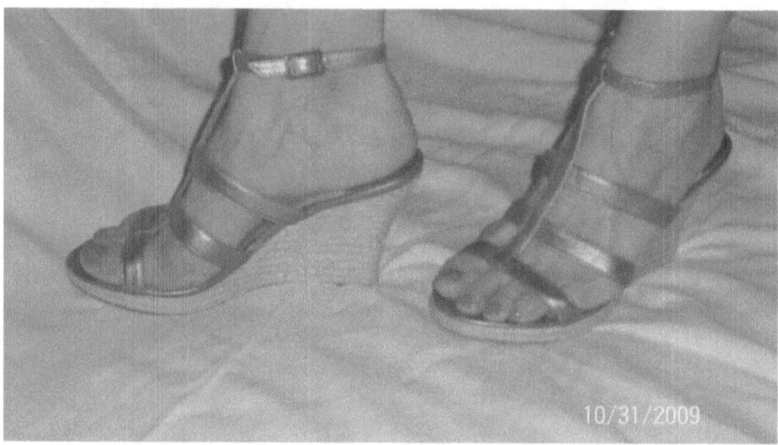

These come in various abbreviations of the sandal with the thick wedge sole. Remember guys, the thick wedge sole; hence wedges. They are good for all seasons and are regarded as both casual and dressy shoes.

KITTEN HEELED SANDALS

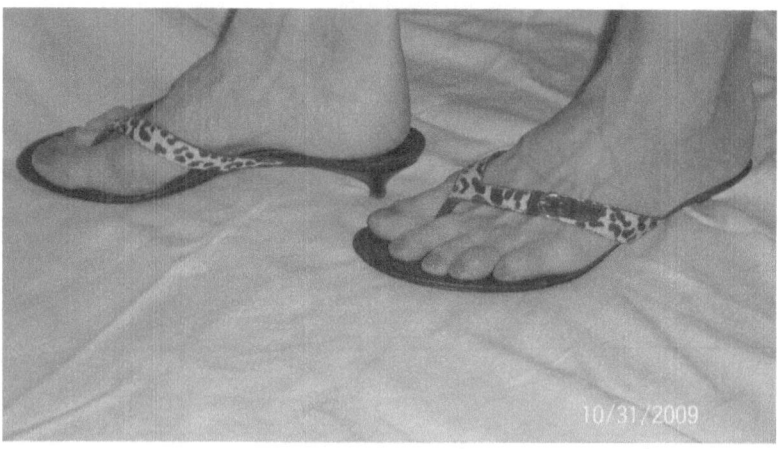

Again these come in various abbreviations and designs. They have the small heel which makes them sexy but functional. Good for casual days in the summer where comfort is primarily the focus.

WEDGE PEEPTOE

The wedge is pronounce but these are regarded as dressy shoes for work, in all seasons; depending on the weather.

SLING BACKS

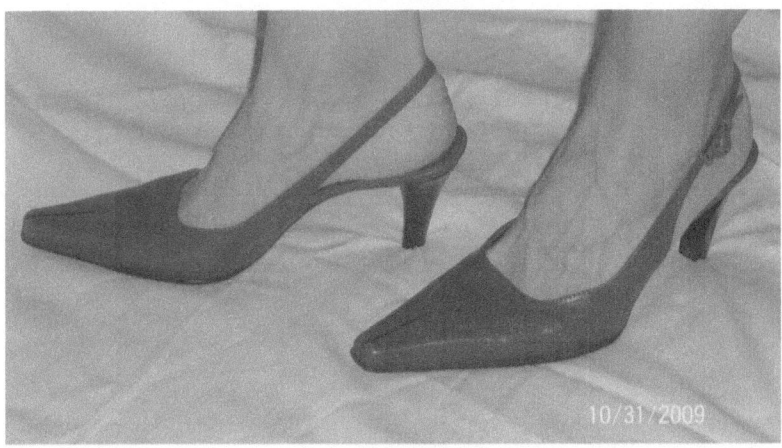

A traditional dressy shoe, which comes in various abbreviations. Looks good with a nice business outfit, or pair of jeans.

CLOGS

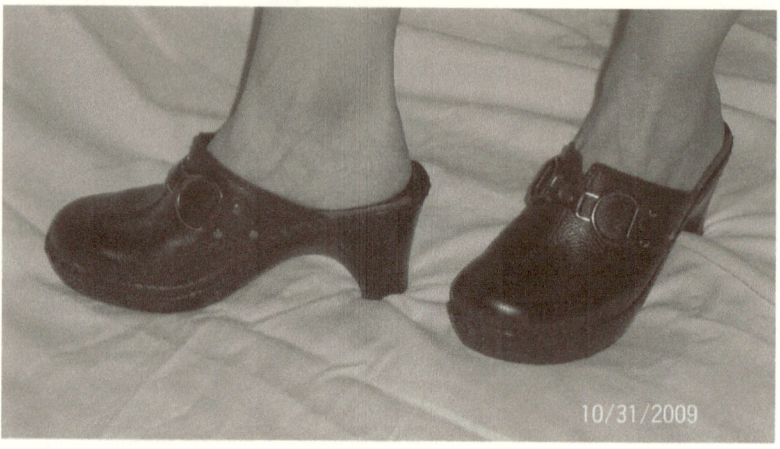

Comfort shoes that are mostly for casual wear. Come in various abbreviations, but are functional for walking and can be worn in winter with stockings or socks.

STRAPPY SANDALS

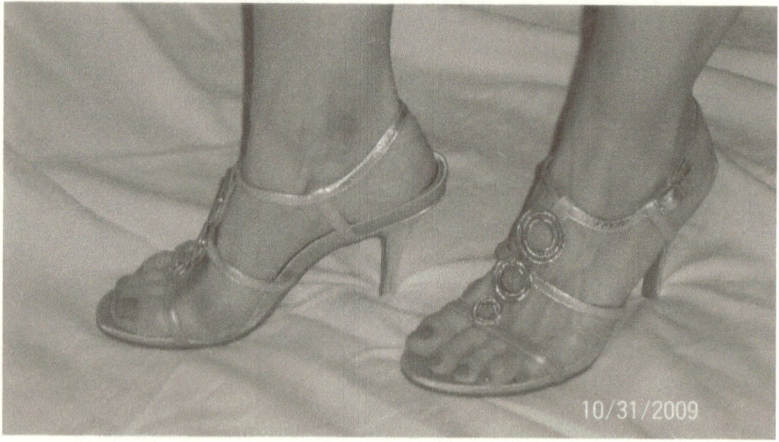

The sexy strappy sandals are for those days during summer on hot days, where loose fitting clothing is primarily the focus. A good shoe to be worn on nights out, as they express something.

BOOTS

The good old sexy boots that come in various lengths. The abbreviations are mainly the heels. The chunky cowboy boot, the flat horse riding heel, pointed toes or without. Nothing beats a good boot; and especially the ones that go above the knee.

PEEPTOE PLATFORM MULES

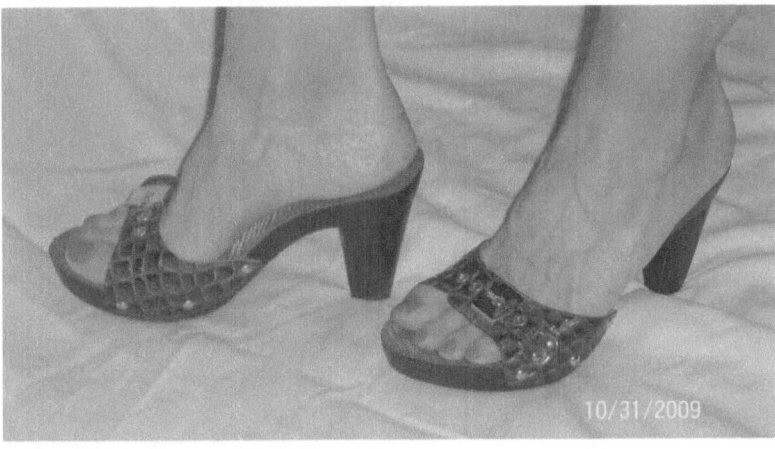

These are the classic combination of a platform and a mule, with the sexy peeptoe. Men beware when she is wearing these..

MULES

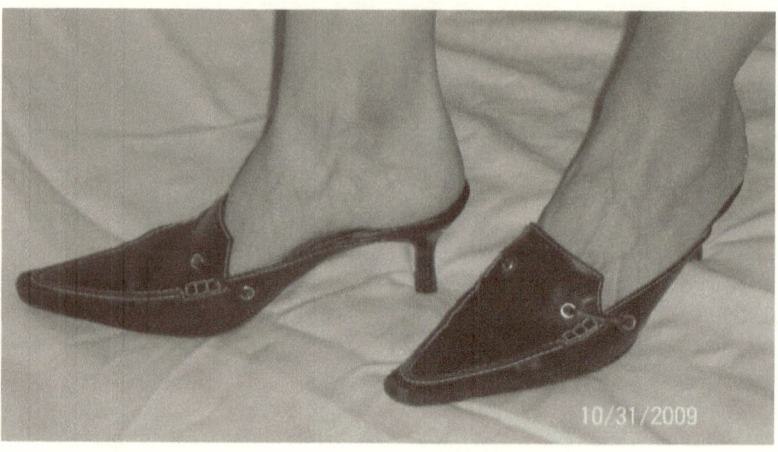

Mules are a dressy shoe that can be worn with a nice pants outfit

PEEPTOE PUMPS

Come in various abbreviations, but a shoe that goes well with a nice dress or pants.

CHUNKY HEEL SANDALS

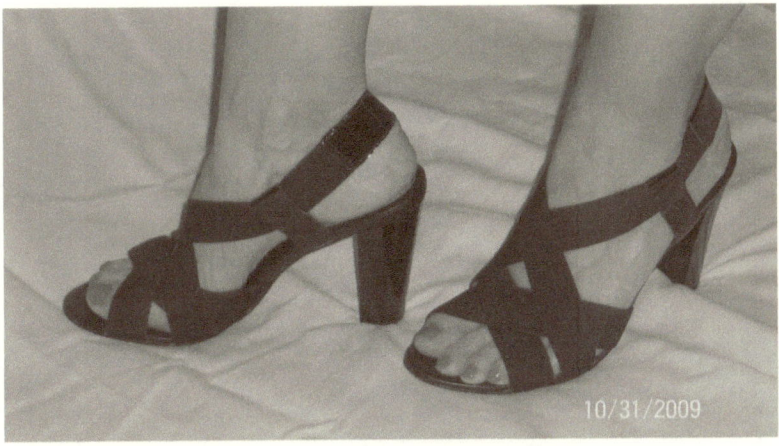

A great all round shoe that can be worn casual or dressy.

PUMPS

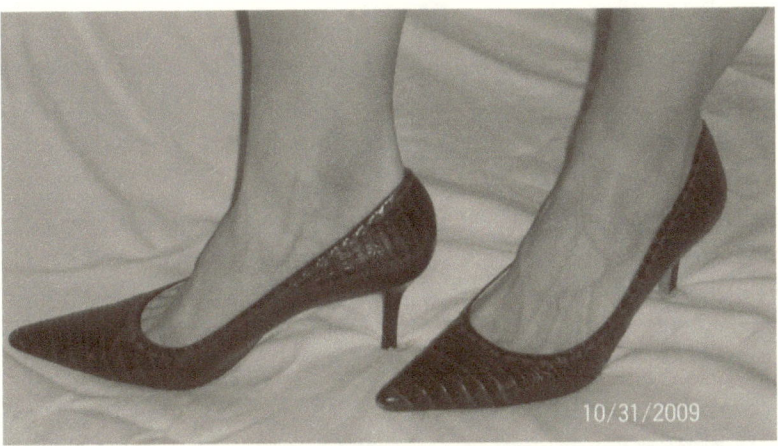

The dress shoe that comes in various abbreviations but looks great with any formal outfit.

BOOTIES

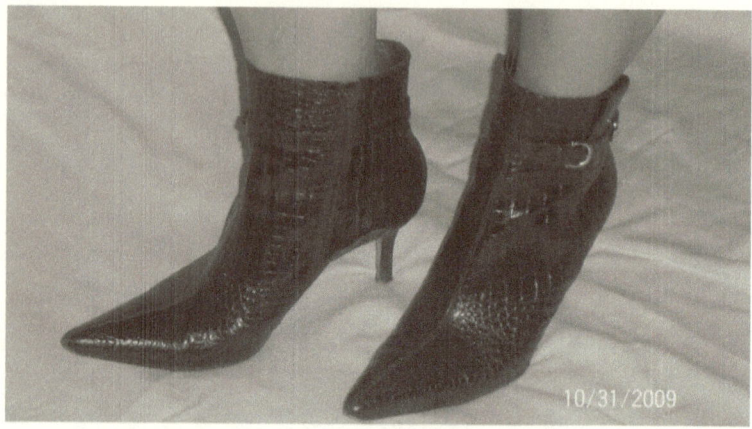

The fun shoe for those winter days when she needs to dress up, but at the same time be frivolous.

As you can see the names are imaginative, and I praise the designers of these shoes; as they must have limited imaginations in coming up with the dialogue of inventory.

I would like to see a more outrageous terminology, like…"that's a nice pair of doggies, pooches, flat-bottoms, skiffs….. and so on. Let's go to my website and create a whole new terminology (dictionary) of women's shoes.

I feel that woman's shoes can be transformed into a stricter categorization; as there are so many abbreviations. To keep women happy and contented in life, we have to keep on designing shoes of different shapes, sizes, configurations and colors.

The next big craze will be "GREEN SHOES," or recycled shoes. We could even consider more dramatic trends; where we take an about turn and go back to the dark ages and "pre-historia." Prehistoric shoes, where the woman sows a piece of leather around her feet.

No…., I don't think so!!!! I can't see my baby princess slipping on a piece of deer hide in the morning.

WHAT TYPE OF SHOES DOES SHE OWN?

This is a hard one trying to determine the personality of a woman based on her shoes; however I believe there is a direct correlation to the type of woman and the type of shoes. I am no psychologist, but I have made assumptions based on my observation of women.....and there are a lot to observe.

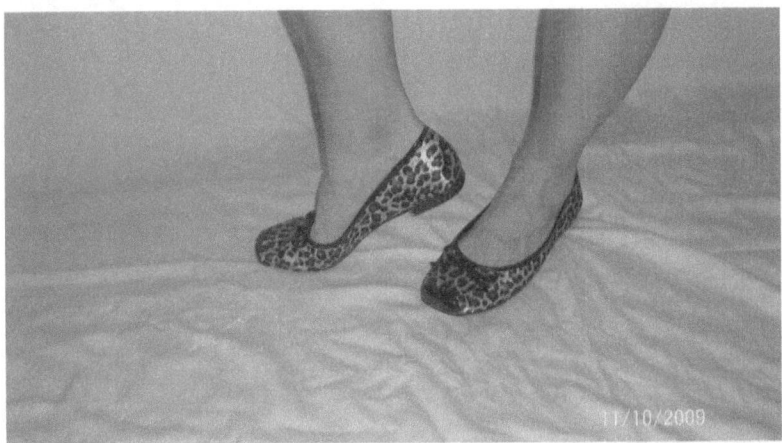

FLATS

I have observed that a woman who predominantly wears flats is normally tall, slender and with a hint of shyness. She is confident in the fact that she is tall, and is her equal with most men; knowing that she is on their level so to speak. However, there is a hint of insecurity; and she will occasionally put on those stilettos to exert her stature when she is in the company of a lot of men. Looking down gives her that confidence. When she wears those flats you will normally see the cuffs folded over, but they are ready to be un-folded when she leashes her dominance and puts on those 4 inch stilettos.

10/31/2009

PUMPS

A woman who wears those thick heeled/soled pumps is normally a petite slender build woman who needs the "pump," to bring her up to the level of the men around her. She is normally a very confident and determined woman, who walks with assertion and commands respect because she has a lot of kicking power between her soles and the ground

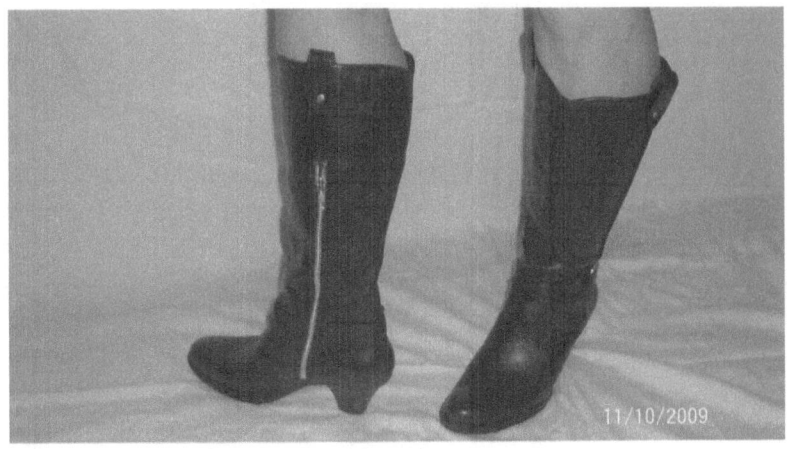

BOOTS

A woman who wears boots is normally carefree, relaxed and does not place a lot of emphasis on the shoe wardrobe. Now this relates to women who wear boots on a regular basis; not the woman who puts on boots occasionally. The woman wearing boots on a regular basis does not care about elevating her stature, and there is very little height in the heel. However, the woman wearing boots occasionally, has a masterpiece; a boot that stands out in the crowd. When you look at her you see nothing but boot, like a Gestapo goddess; that's why all us men have had a fascination with boots.

STILLETTOS

I have always made the correlation of stiletto heels to the length of the dress/skirt that the woman is wearing. The women I have observed wearing stilettos normally have a skirt that is the equivalent number of inches above the knee. "The longer the stilettos, the shorter the skirt."

I have tried to ascertain the meaning of this…. " Look at how long my legs are?" Because that is really all you see, stilettos and legs.

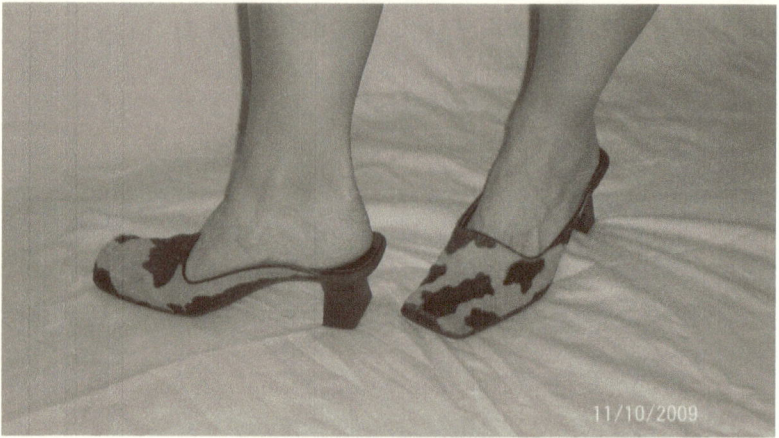

11/10/2009

MULES

Mules, the classic TMDFMQ shoes in my opinion!! No correlation to the hairy four legged beast; which we all interpret as having the brain of a pea; but maybe some of the women wearing these shoes, have the same stubbornness associated with these animals? Only joking, don't forget a man wrote this book.

DO THEY TALK TO HER?

I have frequently gone shopping with my little princess and might add it is a laborious task trying to keep up with her as she darts around the aisles. I have stood silently in the wings trying to blend in with the architecture; leaning on a clothes rack, up against a pillar or sitting in the corner like a child waiting for his mama. " You all know what we look like," and each one of us has a different technique for blending in. We all have one thing in common....We are the laborers carrying all the shopping bags.

I have always wondered how my baby hones in on a specific item that catches her eye. Is it built in radar? A computer based program that she places in her head, and marches through the aisles, zoning in on the article that catches her eye? I have seen her walk through a department store and a hundred feet away see a particular shoe buried in a heap of shoes on a clearance rack; and make a dash to investigate.

My question is; "Do they talk to her?" The next time you have the privilege to go shopping with your better half, closely observe her focus and blank look on her face. It appears there are a thousand voices going through her mind, and that is why I say the shoes talk to her.

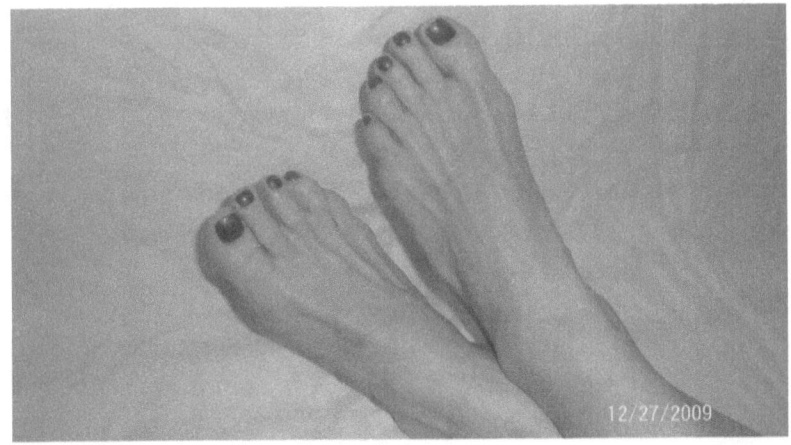

12/27/2009

WOMENS FEET DICTATE THE TYPE OF GAL SHE IS....

We all come in various sizes and models...like a car; there are slender sleek models, and the then there's the beetle, round and about.

I believe there is a correlation to the size of a woman and the shape and size of her feet. This correlation dictates the type and style of shoes she wears.

A three hundred pound woman may not feel appropriate in wearing four inch stilettos, as this is a structural issue. They will seek out shoes that are more appropriate for evenly distributing the weight. However, it is my belief that if shoe manufacturers were more attuned to the needs of the larger woman, they would fashion a sexy stiletto heeled shoe that had the structural integrity to support the larger fairer sex. I feel these women predominately wear flats.

The opposite is the bean stalk, who is small petite and would blow over in a thirty mile wind. Unfortunately these women are relegated to wearing a lot of sport shoes, flats and boots. Their subconscious tells them that they would not look good in stilettos, or pumps; and they can only express their frame in a select style of shoes.

The all round woman, who has shape but well proportioned. This woman wears all the different types of shoes, and looks good in all of them. It is unfortunate though that the shoe manufacturers focus on this category of woman, and leave out those women that are in between.

What type of feet does she have? You have the slender long toes that I assimilate to a gazelle. You have the small pudgy feet that I assimilate to a little piggy. Personally I like little piggy's. Then you have the larger broader and more voluptuous feet that I assimilate with a Clydesdale.

Whatever feet you have they are all sexy, and a woman knows that there is a pair of shoes out there that makes her feet look like gold, and feel a million dollars. Shoes make a woman, not the woman making the shoes look good.

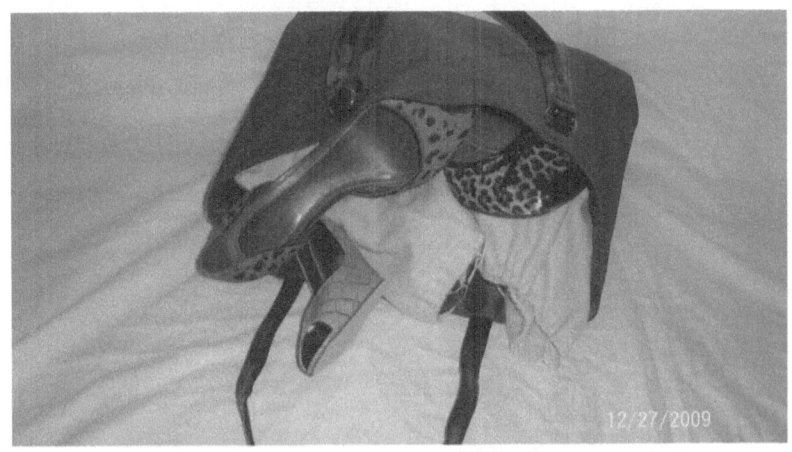

12/27/2009

DOES SHE HIDE HER SHOE PURCHASES OR SHARE THEM?

This is a difficult one to answer, as all answers differed in my questionnaire. However, the general consensus was that women tended to hide their shoe purchases from their significant other.

That being said, 'the significant other was usually a married spouse and not a live-in-boyfriend or casual acquaintance.' The married women all tended to hide their shoes, and there were some interesting answers to the question. The single women tended not to care if their boyfriends noticed new shoes or not. Perhaps it has something to do with the household budget.

In our earlier analysis we determined the estimated expenditure on shoes over a woman's expected lifetime of purchases. Hence, from a man's perspective that would be a new house or a thousand set's of golf clubs? I think that's why women tend to hide their shoe purchases.

In my own experience, my baby always hides her shoe purchases. I try and stake out the front door to see a new bag or box coming into the house, but I have never been able to see them arrive. I always see them being worn, and hence they are no longer new shoes. Occasionally, I might catch the smell of new leather in the morning, and then I know that I have witnessed a major event. The first day they are being worn, like breaking in a new bronco.

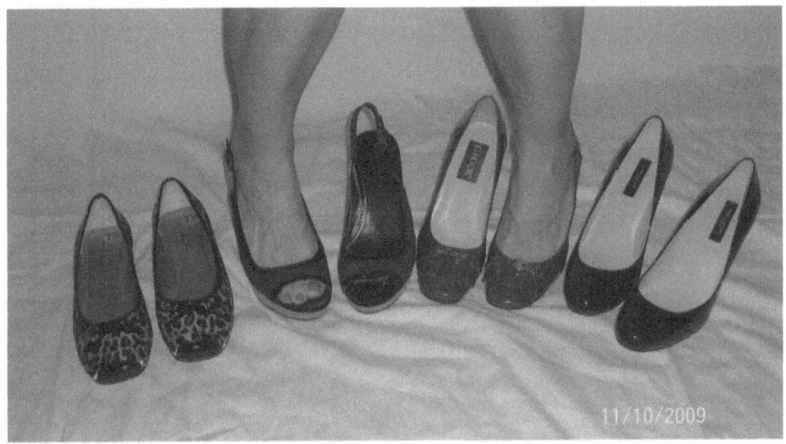

HOW SHE DECIDES WHAT SHOES TO WEAR?

The questionnaire was revealing in that the general consensus was that "COLOR" was the first choice in dictating what shoes to wear. I presume this does not apply to the poor ladies who are color blind.

The second most apparent choice was style, as it related to the outfit they were wearing that day.

Lastly, it was the mood they were in that particular morning....I know as it relates to my wife, she needs plenty of coffee in the mornings to get the motor running, to make that perfect hair-do!!! Women and their hair dryers, god-bless the Chinese for making our babies function each day.

I know from experience, the days that don't start too well, because I made the coffee too weak; the mood is not right and hence the effort to find the perfect color, style and mood of shoe is disrupted. That's when you find a lot of shoes scattered around the dresser, because it takes even more effort to find the perfect fit, so to speak. I generally pick up the pieces after she has left and stash the babies in a tidy order, so my princess can put them back in their appropriate order in the closet. I would never dare to try and organize the shoes in the closet.

For all the men out there, heed my warning…Her shoes are a very personal thing, so there are places you go; and places you don't go.

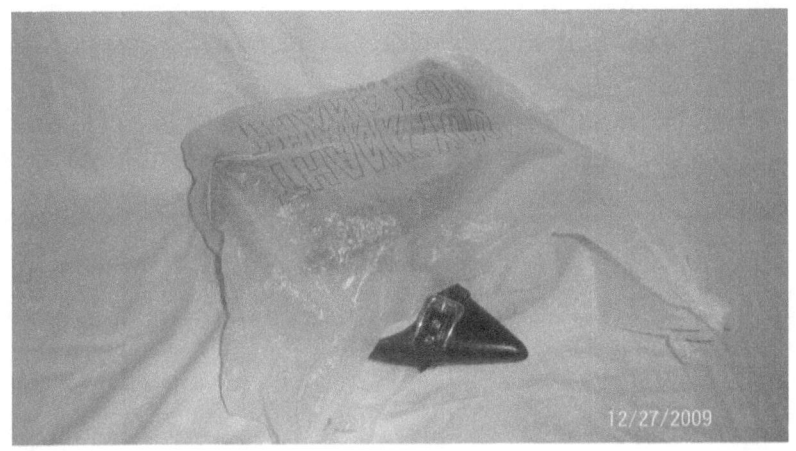

12/27/2009

HOW LONG DOES SHE KEEP HER SHOES ?

Researching my wife, she says she keeps her shoes until:-

a) They are no longer useful,

b) They are no longer in style,

c) They tend to hurt her feet,

They are no longer repairable (which I believe is a fallacy) as I have never seen a bill from the shoe doctor,

Or, as she honestly admits; she needs to make room for a new pair that catches her eye,

I tend to believe that answer (5) applies to all women, as when I have been doing my research and staring at all the shoes passing me by, I have never seen an old pair of shoes. They all look brand new out of the box; not like us men who have scuffs, worn soles and those tell tale leather wrinkles that show up on a worn pair of shoes.

Women's shoes do not have any wrinkles, they are smooth as a baby's bottom; and I think all women will agree that they honestly do not have a pair of old shoes.

When you analyze my wife's schedule of shoe rotations, the numbers are interesting. She admits that she has one pair that she wears about twice a week, because:-

The shoes are comfortable,

The shoes are stylish and go with everything,

These are a pair of peep toe chunky heeled sandals. Poor baby's, they are worn about 104 days of the year..

She admits that the rest of the shoes are worn about 4-6 times a year, which depends on how much inventory she has at any one time. Hence, 40, 50 or 60 pairs of shoes would mean they are worn the mean average 4-6 times.

I would think that most women would fit into this category. They have the odd shoes that they may keep for 6-8 years, but honestly speaking these are shoes that are worn maybe once or twice a years. These baby's don't even have any tread marks on the soles, or as a man would put it they are like 1000 mile tires.

How long do you keep your shoes? That is the question we would all like to know. I think shoe manufacturers of the world, would also like to know; because they are all going strong keeping up with the demand.

WHERE DO THEY ALL GO?

A rhetorical question, as we would all like to know where they disappear to. Where does all the leather go? I have been in a business where I frequented the landfills on a weekly basis, and never did I see a pair of women's shoes in the pile of rubbish. Maybe there was the odd pair that I disposed of from the debris I had picked up, but there was never any quantity.

I know that the thrift stores are overwhelmed with women's shoes, and that a lot are circulated among the not so lucky women; who cannot afford to buy their pair of $200 designer shoes.

One of our survey participants admitted giving shoes to her maid who in turn handed them onto friends and associates. Maybe, the reality is that all these shoes end up in third world countries; and hence maybe they don't have the fancy shoe shops that women in the western world are fortunate in having within easy reach.

Wherever they go, we intend to investigate this further; as there should be a service of taking all these shoes and circulating them to the poorer women in third world countries. I think the opportunity exists to put a homing device on a pair of women's shoes, and tracking the little baby's life.

It would be an interesting epilogue to the saga of "where do they all go?"

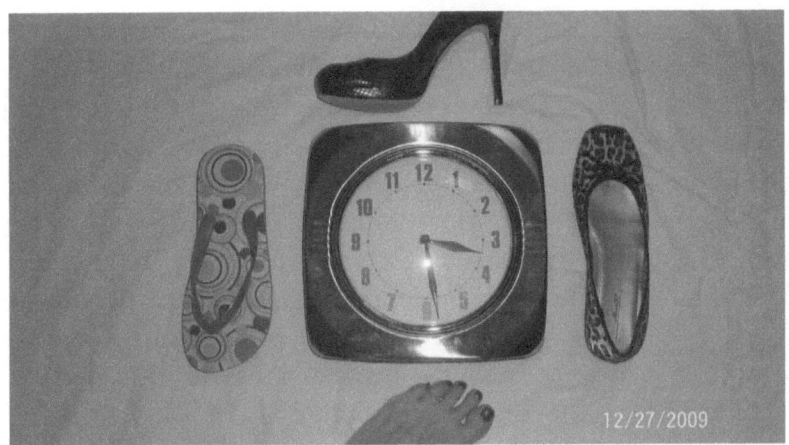

THE SIN CITY SURVEY?

I recently had the opportunity to visit Sin City, Las Vegas with my wife on a business trip.

I don't gamble, but enjoy my golf; so I had two pleasurable rounds on some of the local courses. However, as I am always researching my book, I took the opportunity to check out the leather.

Now this is seeing women at their finest; going to Sin City for fun, frolicking, excitement and whatever else tickles their fancy? They are in the mental framework to wear a whole range of shoes, from flip flops in the spa, to stilettos in the nightclubs; and I am sure their bags were full to accommodate their various endeavors.

While I was waiting for my meager bags to come off the carousel, a woman beside me was being assisted by a porter who was unloading her three bags. "Two bags of clothes, and as she put it; one sizeable bag of shoes." We all know what she will be doing; having lots of fun!!!!!

Now, the daily transition is quite interesting, watching the cycle of shoes being worn. In the early mornings when I wandered down to get my coffee at 6.00am; I watched women coming back to the hotel from a night on the town; climbing out of the limos. Quite a sight, and from a man's perspective it looked like a herd of cows that had just come out of the milking barn. You could see that these women were dragging their feet and stumbling awkwardly, as they were wearing the sexiest, most uncomfortable shoes they could find. They had been dancing the night away in these stilettos, and their poor little "piggy's" were probably screaming. I could hear the squeals, as they made their way through the front of the hotel; and that's when they are all doing the 'drag my feet slide.' Like a Japanese Geisha walk.

Staying longer around the lobby, you then see the flip flop crowd around 11.00am, coming down to get coffee and breakfast. The younger women 20-40 wear flip flops and flats; the older women 40-80 tended to be a little more "well-dressed" as you put it, wearing sandals, clogs, and more comfortable but dressy shoes. I also saw a lot of the older women in their sneakers, probably prescriptions from their podiatrist.

The cycle goes on, around 4.00pm to 7.00pm, you saw the shoes getting better and better. That's when they slip on the comfortable fancy shoes to go to happy hour, or grab a few hours in the casino. The dollar value of the shoes grew more, as the hours passed away.

Finally, around 10.00pm, that's when the real butt kicking fancy feet appeared. The TMDFMQ shoes, (next chapter) came out. Yes, there were some fancy shoes and boots. High heels are definitely back in style, as I said earlier; the higher the heel, the shorter the dress. My only comment is that I feel sorry for the women who have to put on these night owl shoes and wear them for 6-8 hours. It's a chore to get laid, and a painful, laborious task to prance around showing your stuff; and your shoes?

 My final research was at the Las Vegas airport as I had four hours to kill while I waited with all the other zombies for my flight.

Watching the women come and go, I broke down the percentages as follows:-

1. Thirty percent were wearing flip flops,

2. Thirty percent were wearing flats,

3. Twenty percent were wearing boots,

4. Ten percent were wearing sneakers,

5. Ten percent were in assorted low heeled sandals,

It was amazing as I could hear all the feet breathing a sigh of relief. Thank you baby, we are on our way home; and whatever just happened in Vegas is going to stay in Vegas!!!

TMDFMQ.......SHOES?

Now you are all wondering about my interpretation or abbreviation for TMDFMQ Shoes. It means, "Throw me down and F... me quick shoes."

Yes, it is my belief that all women have a pair of these shoes hidden away in their closet for those days and mostly nights when they need to put them to use.

When I look at my wife, I believe she has various pairs; but that's just my imagination getting the better of me. I believe all men need to hunt out the pair that fits the bill. Boy's, you need to check out that beauty that walks in the room; but first look at her shoes.

If the shoe fits, " so to speak; " then you maybe in luck?

Now it could be a sexy pair of boots, or more appropriately a pair of sexy sandals. I believe the peep-toe platform mules are definitely the TMDFMQ shoes. They slip on and off quickly, and can still be worn when in full action.

Another pair that fits the bill are definitely the stilettos, and as I said earlier; the longer the heel the shorter the dress. It is my belief that all men have a fascination with these shoes, and our imaginations get the better of us. The only downfall, is that they can be dangerous.

Whatever the shoes, there is always a pair of TMDFMQ shoes around to keep us boy's happy.

So when you are dating that one and only beauty in your life, watch the shoes. One day she is going to put on that special pair of baby's; that is your ticket to be the only time that you have the privilege of taking them off, or keeping them on. "Maybe you will also be wearing them, so to speak."

TRYING TO UNDERSTAND THE PSYCHOLOGY OF WOMEN AND SHOES?

From a man's perspective I think this is the million dollar question. Where did this originate in the evolution of the woman?

Going through time you first had bare feet, when woman were chased around the camp fire during the stone-age. I don't think there was any particular adornment on their feet.

Taking a jump forward, the next phase was probably stitched hides that covered their feet..... deer, bear, antelope, and saber-tooth. This is probably where the fashion sense first originated. If you had saber-tooth; that was equivalent to your Manolo blahniks, or Jimmy Choo's.

Then came the boots that all women wore; along with their ten layers of clothes that were draped to the floor. I feel this is where the transition happened. Removing those layers of clothes, corset and under-garments opened up a whole new opportunity; as their feet were now exposed.

A smart shoe-maker probably in Europe or Asia came up with the idea of decorating the shoes, as they were very visible. Woman's fascination with shoes began.

However, the interest begins when they are two, three years old; rummaging around in their mother's closet. I would hasten to guess that 90% of women have a fascination with shoes, and hence this cycle goes on and on. Young girls check out those shoes at an early age. As was reported by one of the surveys, she started wearing and exploring those fabulous shoes her aunt use to wear. It followed her into adulthood.

This whole cycle is now emphasized by the amount of children's shoes that are on offer in the shops. If you visit the stores, the section dedicated to young girls is growing and growing.

I asked my wife, why do you like shoes? She confessed that shoes were more important than clothes, because:-

1. Even when you're having a bad hair day, wearing a great pair of shoes makes everything o.k.

2. Putting on a new pair of shoes is like driving a new car every day.

3. Even when you have gained five pounds, wearing a great pair of shoes still makes you feel sexy.

4. A fabulous pair of shoes gives you great confidence.

5. A woman dealing with the daily necessities and chores of life. I.e. Husband, kids, dogs, work; can put on her favorite pair of shoes, and forget who she is?

Finally, men are not absolved with having a fascination with shoes. However, we are focused on one style of shoes, and that would be the sneaker. Men will pay hundreds for a fancy sneaker that has some celebrity name adorned on the side. I don't know if it's the sneaker we really like, or the feeling that when we put it on; we become the celebrity who wears them.

I think the press could go a long way to exploiting this, if they promoted what male celebrities were wearing on their feet; and then maybe we would have a revolution in the male footwear category. Naming these shoes after the country singers, football players, actors, (we have already had basketball and golf) would spark a revival in the shoe economy for men.

MY CONCLUSIONS?

Whatever makes you happy; makes all of us men happy in life. Because our lives are a lot happier when you're happy!!

Shoes make women happy, and they will continue to have this fascination for eons to come; as the cycle starts the minute they put on their first little booties.

I hope this book and our website will offer a sanctuary for women to share their joy and appreciation for all these shoes. A public forum to express themselves, and to explore the many new shoe opportunities!

We also feel that the live modeling of shoes will allow all of you to see "if the shoe fits, so to speak." We are not manufacturers or retailers; we are an independent forum for you to express what you feel about new shoes, and for you to give honest opinions.

1. Do they fit well?
2. Do they hold up to wear?
3. Are they comfortable?

Questions and answers, all women will appreciate from their peers.

For the men in this world, read the book and visit the website. It will give you a better appreciation of the most important person in your life; if your partner is a woman. She may have fancy clothes; fancy handbags; (another book) and a whole lot of jewelry; but the shoes are one of her most prized possessions.

Thank you for sharing this fun, lighthearted journey into the realm of women's shoes!!!